A little dose

of Positivity

Teresa D. Richardson

A Dose of Positivity

All bible verses in this book are from the New King James Version.

ISBN NO. 978-1-943409-75-4.

Printed in the United States of America

Pure Thoughts Publishing LLC

A Dose of Positivity

Table of Contents

A Dose of Positivity

In a world that's full of violence, negativity, and sometimes uncertainty, it's always good to have a positive ray of sunshine to brighten up your day. It is amazing how one positive thought can change your entire day. Truth is, we all have the power to set the tone for our lives. Each day, we unwrap this precious gift called LIFE and it's up to us to make the most of every moment. My goal is to live a positive lifestyle. I want to find something good in every situation I encounter whether good or bad. Many people around the world are dealing with low self-esteem, anxiety, depression, and so many other things that have been controlling us for so long. God desires us to be free, and to be truly happy from the inside out. If you think positive, it will help you achieve happiness and contentment. Positivity will motivate you to accomplish anything you set your mind to.

A Dose of Positivity

POSITIVITY
IS THE

Dear Friend,

My prayer is that this book is the ray of sunshine that you have been looking for. I want to motivate you with a dose of positivity, a platform to set your goals and follow through, deal with the things we struggle with head on and resolve them, and to empower your mind by repeating daily affirmations an reading daily scriptures to spice up your day. I hope you enjoy this little book of positivity!

-Teresa Richardson

A Little Dose of Positivity

Once you replace negative thoughts with positive, you will see positive results. Here's a few positive thoughts to brighten up your life.

A reason for everything

There is a lesson in everything that we go through. The key to it is learning from our mistakes and applying wisdom as you continue to grow.

Giving up vs letting go

Giving up is not fighting anymore for something that is worth fighting for. Letting go is walking away from something or someone that is hurting you, destroying your spirit, your self esteem and who you are as a person.

I often hear people say the "struggle is real"

I often hear people say the struggle is real. I agree and today I pray for you. Every soul that is struggling with illnesses and diseases, dealing with strongholds and addictions, self esteem issues, depression, fear, confusion, and those that are at the end of their rope. I pray that God breaks the chains that have you bound and I speak healing, deliverance, peace, and total freedom from everything the enemy has placed in your life in the name of Jesus! Be free! Yes, the struggle is real, but the God that I serve is real and he is able to break EVERY chain!

In everything, give thanks

We often become too relaxed in our lives that we begin to take things for granted. In everything, give thanks. Some of the best gifts you will ever receive are priceless. Life, health, strength, ability to see, hear, walk, and talk. Some people don't possess those things. You are blessed. You may not have as much as the next person but be grateful for what you have and the positive people that you are connected to. Life is a vapor. You can be here today and gone tomorrow. I challenge you to tell someone you love them and give thanks for everything.

Just in case you forgot...

Always remember that God loves you. Sometimes it takes time, patience, and faith for things to improve. Place yourself in his hands and before you know it, things will be better. Believe in yourself and trust that God has it all under control.

Each day is a gift!

Each day is a fresh start. It is up to make the most of every moment of your day. One positive thought can change your entire day. Think positive, talk positive, and watch how awesome your day is. You got this!

Stand up, my friend!

Struggles are required to survive in life. In order to stand up, you have to know what falling down is like. Stand up, my friend. Keep going! God has your back!

Reflections

Begin each day with something positive. Set the bar high, and the rest of your day will be awesome! It's a mind thing! Think positive, speak positive, live a positive lifestyle.

Help is on the way!

Hey, you! Guess what? It is perfectly okay to ask for help. Yes! It is! Sometimes we get overwhelmed with the details and complexities of our lives. Sometimes we need some help to get untangled, but we often let our pride or inner fears stop us from asking for help. In this season, my friend, you need to know that it is okay to ask for help. The answer to your earnest prayers could be right under your nose.

A Dose of Positivity

Be still and know

Some people relax with television, some people curl up with a good book, and some relax with friends. But when was the last time you rested by truly doing nothing? Think about it! Sometimes it is necessary to simply "be still" and breathe. Take out time for YOU. It's perfectly okay to REST.

Don't sit on it

Don't let life pass you by. One of my favorite quotes was "If you do something you love, no one has to motivate you." Don't sit on the couch and wait for it. Make a change! Smile more, be excited. Do something new. Unfollow negative people on social media. Be fierce! Show gratitude. Do things that challenge you. If you want different results, you have to change some things! Don't allow fear to paralyze you. Don't sit on it, Step out on faith!!

Ready, set, LIVE your best life!

You are equipped with the tools you need to make you life awesome and fulfilling. You have the power to grab each day by the horns and make it the best day of your life! It's a mind thing! Get ready to live your best life! Hold your head up high and smile, because you are one amazing individual!

A Dose of Positivity

It's time to set

your goals

In this section, start the process of setting one or more goals for the month. The process of writing down your goals helps you clarify what you really want to do, understand the importance of pursuing them, and commit yourself to making them happen. It's a mind thing! Set those goals, believe in yourself, and do what it takes to make your dreams a reality. I believe in you!

My Goals for the month

―――――――――――――

Individual Goal#1:

_____

_____

_____

_____

_____

Individual Goal#2:

_____

_____

_____

_____

_____

A Dose of Positivity

Think about ways to reach those goals. Believe in yourself, and you can reach any goal you set.

Notes:

_____

_____

_____

_____

_____

_____

_____

_____

_____

A Dose of Positivity

My Goals for the month of

_____

Individual Goal#1:

_____

_____

_____

_____

_____

Think about ways to reach those goals. Believe in yourself, and you can reach every goal you set.

Individual Goal#2:

_____

_____

_____

_____

_____

A Dose of Positivity

Notes:

_____

_____

_____

_____

_____

_____

_____

_____

_____

_____

_____

A Dose of Positivity

My Goals for the month of

Individual Goal#1:

_____

_____

_____

_____

_____

A Dose of Positivity

Think about ways to reach those goals. Believe in yourself, and you can reach every goal you set in life.

Individual Goal#2:

_____

_____

_____

_____

_____

A Dose of Positivity

Notes:

_____

_____

_____

_____

_____

_____

_____

_____

_____

_____

_____

_____

A Dose of Positivity

My Goals for the month of

_____

Individual Goal#1:

_____
_____
_____
_____
_____

A Dose of Positivity

Think about ways to reach those goals. Believe in yourself, and you can reach every goal you set in life.

Individual Goal#2:

_____

_____

_____

_____

_____

A Dose of Positivity

Notes:

_____

_____

_____

_____

_____

_____

_____

_____

_____

_____

_____

_____

30-day Release: Self-Evaluation

A Dose of Positivity

It's time to evaluate your inner self. What do you struggle with?

What toxic traits do you want to rid yourself of?

Think about it....

Now is the time to face your truth. The longer we carry the weight, the harder it is to be truly happy and free. On the following page, write down one or more things you struggle with. For the next 30 DAYS, pray that God helps you in this area.

We decree a supernatural RELEASE and we embrace your divine FREEDOM from "that thing"! What are you waiting for? BE FREE!

A Dose of Positivity

30 day Release: Self-Evaluation

I Struggle With

_____

_____

_____

_____

_____

_____

_____

A Dose of Positivity

_____

_____

_____

_____

_____

_____

_____

_____

_____

_____

_____

_____

_____

_____

Pray with All Your
Heart Believe with All
Your Soul & You Will
See God Move

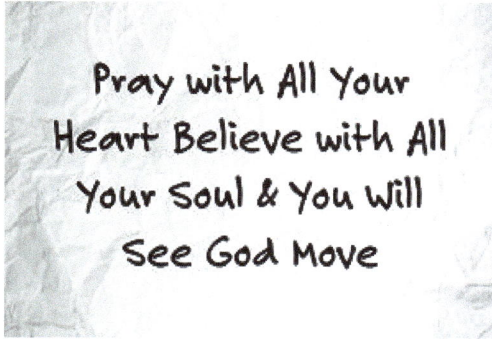

My personal prayer:

Dear Lord, please help me to

_____

_____

_____

_____

_____

A Dose of Positivity

_____

_____

_____

_____

_____

_____

_____

_____

_____

_____

_____

_____

_____

_____

A Dose of Positivity

At the end of my 30 days, I declare that I will no

longer be bound by _____.

30 day Release: Self-Evaluation

I Struggle With

_____

_____

_____

_____

_____

A Dose of Positivity

_____

_____

_____

_____

_____

_____

_____

_____

_____

_____

_____

_____

_____

Pray with All Your
Heart Believe with All
Your Soul & You Will
See God Move

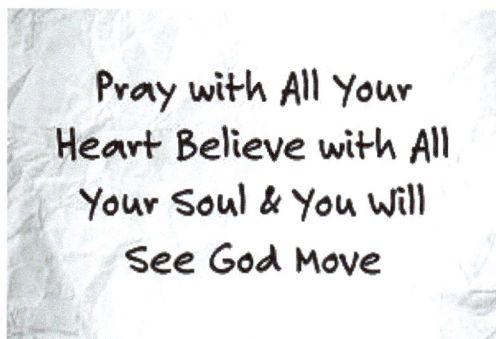

My personal prayer:

Dear Lord, please help me to

_____

_____

_____

_____

_____

_____

_____

A Dose of Positivity

_____

_____

_____

_____

_____

_____

_____

_____

_____

_____

_____

_____

_____

_____

A Dose of Positivity

At the end of my 30 days, I declare that I will no longer be bound by _____.

30-day Release: Self-Evaluation

I struggle with

_____

_____

_____

_____

_____

_____

_____

A Dose of Positivity

_____

_____

_____

_____

_____

_____

_____

_____

_____

_____

_____

_____

A Dose of Positivity

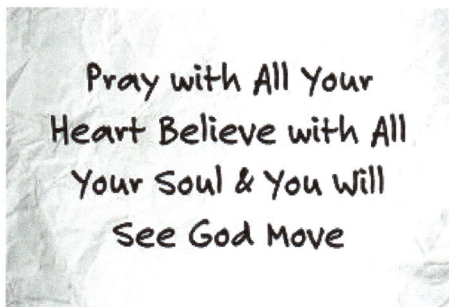

Pray with All Your
Heart Believe with All
Your Soul & You Will
See God Move

My personal prayer:

Dear Lord, please help me to

_____

_____

_____

_____

_____

_____

_____

_____

A Dose of Positivity

_____

_____

_____

_____

_____

_____

_____

_____

_____

_____

_____

_____

Think Positive, Speak Positive

A Dose of Positivity

"Death and life are in the power of the tongue: and they
that love it shall eat the fruit thereof."

Proverbs 18:21

A Dose of Positivity

Daily Affirmations to spice up your day

🌷 Today is a new day. I greet every minute with renewed enjoyment.

🌷 I choose not to stress over things I cannot control.

🌷 I am open to learn something new each day.

🌷 I am the apple of God's eye.

A Dose of Positivity

🌷 I will not allow fear to distract me. I will stay focused.

🌷 I will remain positive in every situation I face.

🌷 All good things are coming to me.

🌷 I have the power to set the tone for my life.

🌷 I am in charge of how I feel. Today, I choose happiness!

🌷 I will not lack.

🌷 I'm attracting positive people into my life with open arms.

A Dose of Positivity

🌷 I am healed, I am healthy, I am whole.

🌷 I radiate unconditional love.

🌷 I am organized and productive.

🌷 I am learning to choose my battles wisely.

🌷 I will spread positivity to everyone I meet today.

🌷 I embrace every opportunity to help others.

🌷 I choose to live my life with no regrets.

🌷 My current situation does not define me.

A Dose of Positivity

🌷 I will complete every goal I set my mind to.

🌷 I am a vibrant soul. I got it going on!

🌷 I accept my flaws and love myself unconditionally.

🌷 I am calm, and relaxed in my mind.

🌷 I am abundantly blessed. I have abundant energy.

🌷 I am forgiven. My past will not control me!

🌷 Everything I speak, I shall have!

A Dose of Positivity

🌷 I will not allow anger to control me.

🌷 I welcome new beginnings in my life.

🌷 My current situation does not define me.

🌷 I will complete every goal I set my mind to.

🌷 I am a vibrant soul. I got it going on!

🌷 I accept my flaws and love myself
unconditionally.

🌷 I am calm, and relaxed in my mind.

A Dose of Positivity

🌷 I am abundantly blessed. I have abundant energy.

🌷 I am forgiven. My past will not control me!

🌷 Everything I speak, I shall have!

🌷 I will not allow anger to control me.

🌷 I welcome new beginnings in my life.

Uplifting Scriptures designed to help you along the way.

Dear Friend,

Whether you need a boost of courage or an infusion of motivation, we can turn to the word of God for just the right counsel. May the words of God bless your heart.

A Dose of Positivity

"So shall the knowledge of wisdom be unto thy soul; when thou hast found it, then there shall be a reward, and thy expectation shall not be cut off".

Proverbs 24:14

"For I know the thoughts that I think towards you, saith the Lord, thoughts of peace, and not of evil, to give you an expected end." -Jeremiah 29:11

"And hope maketh not ashamed; because the love of God is shed abroad in our hearts by the Holy Ghost which is given to us." -Romans 5:5

"The Lord shall preserve thee from all evil: he shall preserve thy soul. The Lord shall preserve thy going out and thy coming in from this time forth, and even for ever more.: -Psalm 121:7-8

"I can do all things through Christ which strengthen me.: -Philippians 4:13

A Dose of Positivity

"The Lord is my portion, saith my soul; therefore will I hope in him." -Lamentations 3:24

"And not only so, but we glory in tribulations also; knowing that tribulation worketh patience; and patience, experience; and experience, hope."

 -Romans 5:3-4

"But if we hope for that we see not, then do we with patience wait for it." -Romans 8:25

Blessed is the man that trusteth in the Lord, and whose hope the Lord is." Jeremiah 17:7

"The Lord is all I have, and so in him, I put my hope." -Lamentations 3:24

"While I live will I praise the Lord: I will sing praises unto my God while I have my being."-Psalm 146:2

"Let your hope keep you joyful, be patient in your troubles, and pray at all times." -Romans 12:12

"May the God of hope fill you with all joy and peace as you trust in him, so that you may overflow with hope by the power of the Holy Spirit," -Romans 15:13

"And now these three remain: faith, hope, and love. But the greatest of these is love. -1 Corinthians 13:13

"The Lord is good to all; he has compassion on all he has made." -Psalm 145:9

"For God so loved the world that he gave his only begotten son, that whosoever believeth in him shall not perish, but have everlasting life." John 3:16

"Trust in the Lord with all thine heart and lean not unto your own understanding. In all thy ways, acknowledge him, and he shall direct thy paths." Proverbs 3:5-6

A Dose of Positivity

"Cast all your cares on him because he cares for you." 1 Peter 5:7

Just be yourself.

Let people see the real, imperfect,

flawed, quirky, weird, beautiful, and

magical person that you are. -

Unknwn

A Dose of Positivity

About Author

Teresa Richardson is a wife and mother of four beautiful kids. Born and raised in Bishopville, SC, Teresa has a passion for helping others and being a positive influence in their lives. She is author of "Think on these things" , and social media group facilitator of GirlTalk Women's Empowerment Group, founded by Sharee Peterson. Teresa is also a minister at her church and associate teacher at Darlington County Community Actions Agency. Being positive is her #1 priority and she loves to empower others to live a positive lifestyle.

www.ingramcontent.com/pod-product-compliance
Lightning Source LLC
Chambersburg PA
CBHW041758040426

42447CB00001B/3